W9-AHT-604

SE 1 8 '09

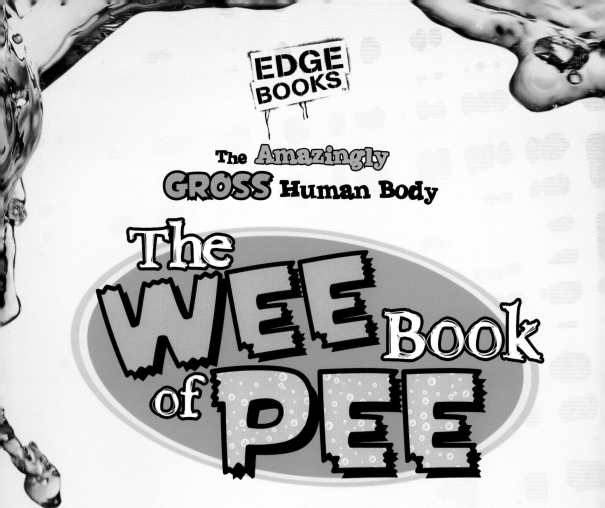

EDGE BOOKS™

The Amazingly GROSS Human Body

The WEE Book of PEE

by Kelly Regan Barnhill

Consultant:
Michael Bentley
Professor of Biology
Minnesota State University, Mankato

Capstone press®

Mankato, Minnesota

Library of Congress Cataloging-in-Publication Data
Barnhill, Kelly Regan
    The wee book of pee / by Kelly Regan Barnhill.
    p. cm. — (Edge books. The amazingly gross human body)
    Includes bibliographical references and index.
    Summary: "Describes the gross qualities of urine, and how it works
to benefit a person's health" — Provided by publisher.
    ISBN 978-1-4296-3357-4 (library binding)
    1. Urine — Juvenile literature. I. Title. II. Series.
QP211.B37 2010
612.4'61 — dc22   2009005054

Editorial Credits
Aaron Sautter, editor; Kyle Grenz, designer; Jo Miller, media researcher

Photo Credits
Alamy/Helene Rogers, 23; The Print Collector, 24; Rob Walls, 11
Capstone Press/Karon Dubke, cover (all), 4, 6 (both), 9, 12, 13, 14, 15,
        17 (top), 18 (inset), 21, 27 (inset), 28, 29
Getty Images Inc./3D4Medical.com, 8; David McNew, 26–27;
        DEA Picture Library, 10
Newscom, 20
Peter Arnold/Biosphoto/Lattes Emmanuel, 7
Rainbow/Hank Morgan, 18 (top)
Shutterstock/Filipe B. Varela, borders; Sebastian Kaulitzki,
        17 (bottom)

TABLE of CONTENTS

WHY do we PEE?

Imagine you're sitting in your family's car on a summer trip. The drive is long and boring. You're stuck between your older sister and your drooling baby brother. The road stretches on for miles. There's no gas station or rest area to be seen — and you *really* have to go.

While you're crossing your legs and groaning, a question pops into your head. Why do we pee, anyway? Wouldn't it be easier if we didn't have to pee at all?

PEEING FOR OUR HEALTH

You can't tell by looking at it, but pee, or urine, plays an important role in your health. If you didn't pee, poisons would collect in your muscles, blood, and tissues. You would soon become very sick. Your **organs** would begin to shut down. Without a doctor's help, you'd soon die.

organ — a body part that does a certain job, such as your heart or your lungs

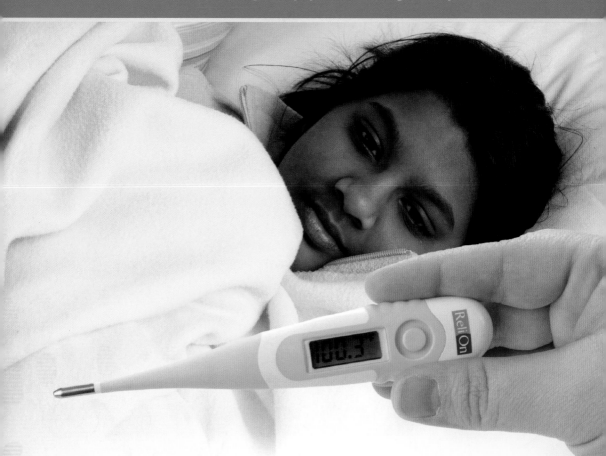

Pee isn't just some stinky yellow stuff people flush down the toilet. The body's cells are constantly making waste products while they work. Something has to clean out all the gunk. Luckily, we have an amazing system of organs that keep our bodies clean and healthy. Let's take a closer look at pee and how it's made.

EVERYBODY PEES

All creatures on earth have to pee. But not all pee looks the same. Fish produce very watery pee that comes out almost constantly. Birds, however, have very thick pee that comes out in a paste.

Desert animals don't pee as much as animals in wetter climates. Some desert animals only pee about once a week. Their pee contains so little water that it comes out a dark brown color.

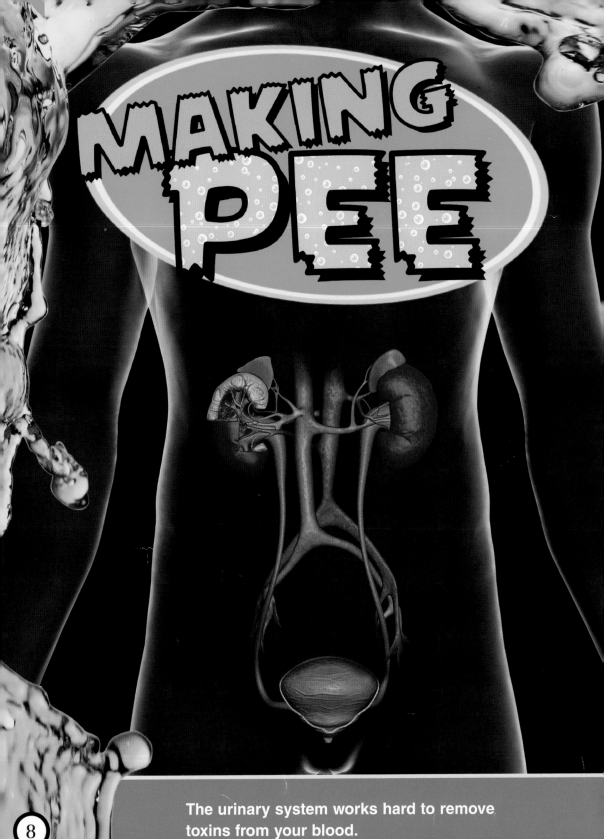

MAKING PEE

The urinary system works hard to remove toxins from your blood.

As you eat, drink, work, and play, your body creates waste products called **toxins**. Your blood carries these toxins through your body until they can be removed. For example, the lungs remove carbon dioxide from your blood so you can breathe it out.

Other poisons are trickier to clean out, though. Thankfully, the human body has the perfect system of organs to clean the blood. It's called the urinary system.

GROSS FACT

Most people produce between 1 and 2 quarts (0.9 and 1.9 liters) of urine every day.

toxin   a poisonous substance

THE AMAZING KIDNEYS

The kidneys are possibly the hardest working organs in your body. These amazing bean-shaped organs sit on both sides of your spine under your ribs. They aren't very big. They're about the same size as your fist. The kidneys have a very important job. As blood passes through them, they trap the poisons that make the body's cells quit working. The kidneys filter your blood many times each day. If you add it up, they filter almost 50 gallons (189 liters) of blood every day!

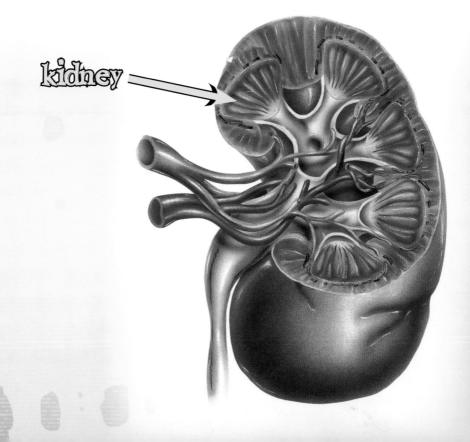

kidney

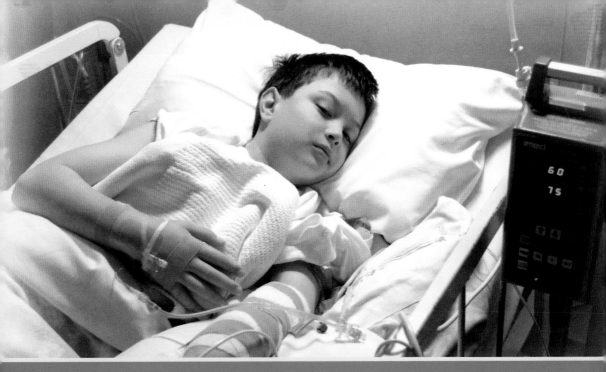

The kidneys also work hard to keep your body in balance, or in **homeostasis**. Your body needs a certain balance of fluids, salts, and other substances to work properly. Water is a good example. If you don't have enough water, you feel thirsty. A little too much, and you can feel bloated. If your body has a lot of excess water, you're at risk of water intoxication. This is a dangerous condition that can cause death if it's not treated right away.

homeostasis — when your body has the right balance of fluids and other substances

THE BODY'S EQUALIZER

Whenever you eat or drink something, you're taking in an acid or an alkaline. Acidity and alkalinity are measured with the pH scale. When something is neutral, like distilled water, it has a pH of 7. Acids have a pH lower than 7. The pH of an alkaline is greater than 7.

A pH tester can show you the acidity or alkalinity of a substance.

Your body's cells need a neutral pH to work properly. Your kidneys work hard to make sure your body doesn't become too acidic or too alkaline. It's a tough job because people are constantly taking in acids and alkalines. For example, when you drink soda, you're drinking an acid. If you eat egg whites, you're eating an alkaline. If your kidneys didn't keep your body's pH balanced, your body would soon begin to shut down and you would die.

WHAT'S IN PEE ANYWAY?

Have you ever noticed how your pee changes color? It can go from pale yellow to a dark, old banana yellow. Why is this? It has a little to do with what you're eating. But it has a lot to do with how much you're drinking. Pee is mostly water. When you drink a lot of water, your pee becomes more diluted and it turns a lighter color.

Pee also contains nitrogen and salt. When you eat, your body's cells use nutrients to provide you with energy. As the nutrients are used, the cells create nitrogen as a waste product. The nitrogen in pee is in the form of urea. Urea is dangerous at high levels. It needs to be removed from the body right away. The kidneys filter out the urea, and it becomes part of your urine. The kidneys also filter out any excess salt that your body can't use.

Your pee is lighter or darker depending on how much water you drink.

A STEADY FLOW

The kidneys never stop working. But all that waste and poison can't just sit in your kidneys. Attached to each kidney is a muscular tube called a **ureter**. These skinny tubes are about as long and thick as a piece of spaghetti. Urine is squeezed through the ureters until it reaches its next stopping point — the bladder.

The bladder is a muscular pouch that collects your pee. As the bladder fills up, it begins to stretch out. Soon, you feel some pressure and get the urge to go to the bathroom. A small muscle at the bottom of the bladder lets you hold the pee until you find a toilet. When it's time to go, the muscle relaxes and the urine flows through your **urethra**, leaving your body.

ureter   one of the small tubes between the kidneys and the bladder

urethra   the small tube that leads to the outside of the body

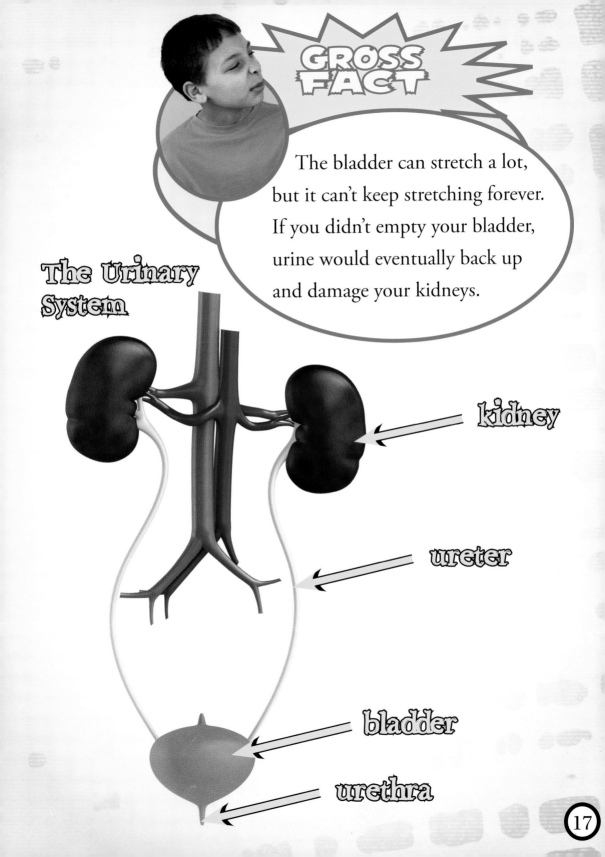

GROSS FACT

The bladder can stretch a lot, but it can't keep stretching forever. If you didn't empty your bladder, urine would eventually back up and damage your kidneys.

The Urinary System

kidney

ureter

bladder

urethra

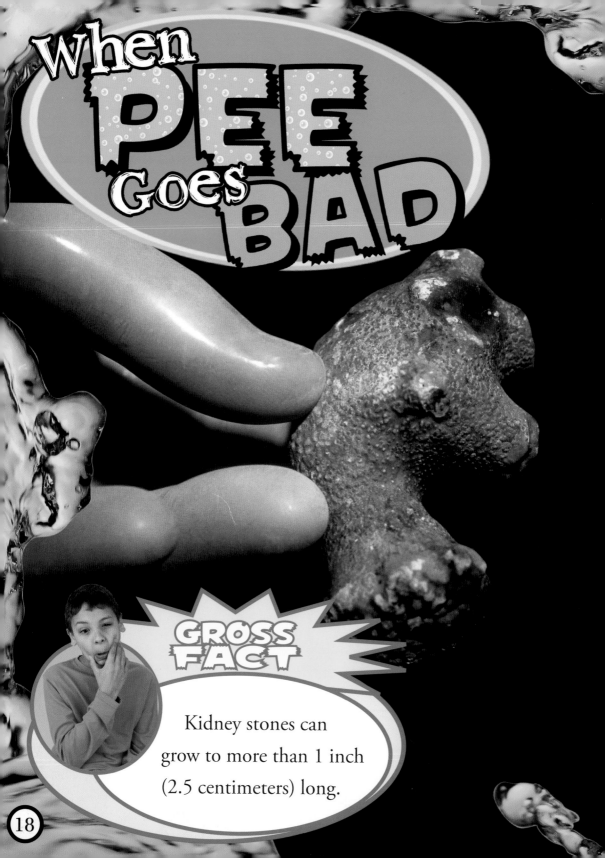

When PEE Goes BAD

GROSS FACT

Kidney stones can grow to more than 1 inch (2.5 centimeters) long.

Most people pee several times a day. They usually don't think about it much. They just pee, flush, and go on with their day. But sometimes, the urinary system doesn't work correctly. When that happens, peeing can be gross and painful. And if your urinary system shuts down completely, pee can even be deadly.

KIDNEY STONES

Sometimes the urea in pee forms tiny crystals inside the kidneys. At first, the crystals are only the size of a grain of sand. And they usually don't hurt — yet.

Over time, the crystals grow bigger. Eventually, the crystals become a kidney stone. People usually don't realize they have a kidney stone until it enters their ureter. When that happens, the stone blocks urine from flowing to the bladder. Meanwhile, the kidneys just keep making more pee. The pressure soon builds up and the kidney begins to swell. The pressure usually causes very intense pain.

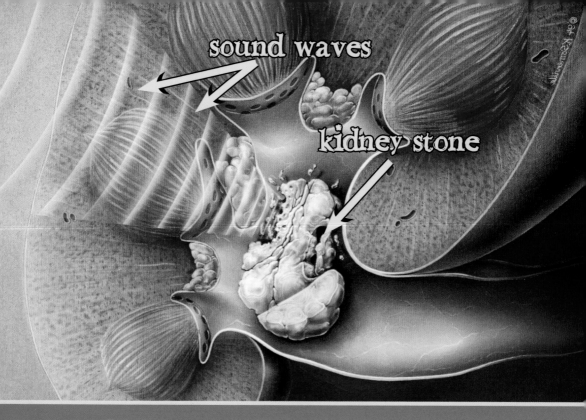

sound waves

kidney stone

Doctors use sound waves to smash large kidney stones into small pieces.

Thankfully, pee comes to the rescue. As pee builds up, it pushes on the stone. Eventually, the stone is pushed into the bladder and out of the body. But some kidney stones grow too large to pass through the body. Doctors often use sound waves to break these large kidney stones into smaller pieces. The small pieces can then pass through the body normally. Occasionally, doctors need to operate to remove especially large stones.

URINARY TRACT INFECTIONS

Sometimes, people feel the urge to pee all the time, even when their bladders are empty. When they do go, it feels like their pee has turned into liquid fire. What's wrong with these people? They probably have a urinary tract infection. Doctors can usually treat urinary infections easily with **antibiotics**. People shouldn't ignore urinary infections. If left untreated, they can cause your kidneys to fail. And if that happens, it can lead to very serious problems.

antibiotic   a drug used to cure infections and disease

KIDNEY FAILURE

Kidneys can break down for several reasons. Infections, **diabetes**, and high blood pressure are just a few. Whatever the cause, doctors have to act quickly. When the kidneys fail, people become very tired. They might start breathing and sweating heavily. Their bodies might swell. If something isn't done quickly, they could die.

People whose kidneys have failed need their blood cleaned regularly. This is done through a process called dialysis. Instead of their kidneys making pee, a machine cleans their blood and pumps it back into their bodies. These patients must go through the process several times each week.

Eventually, the patient will need a new kidney. Sometimes patients can get a new kidney from a relative. But many patients have to wait a long time to get a new one. When they do get a new kidney, patients often say that peeing normally again feels like a miracle. And if you think about it, peeing really is kind of miraculous.

diabetes a disease in which people have too much sugar in their blood

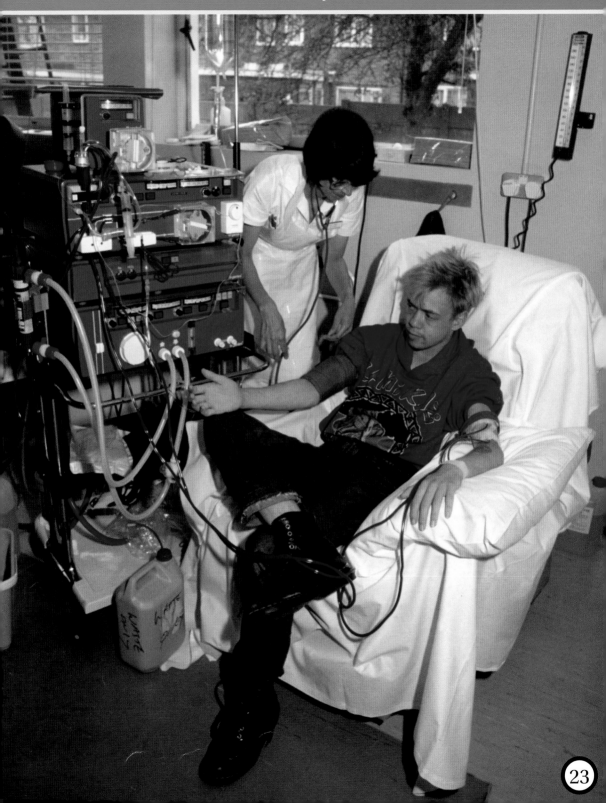

People suffering from kidney failure need their blood cleaned with dialysis treatments.

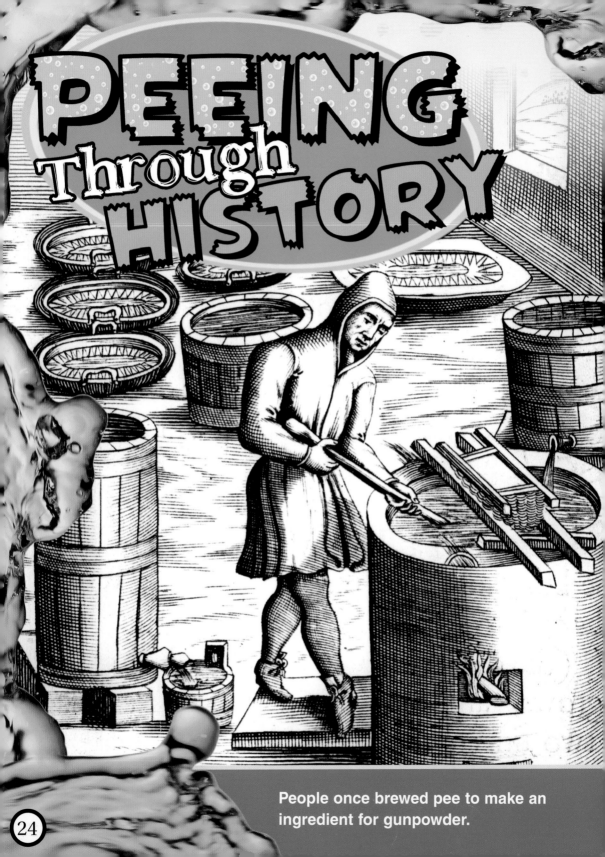

PEEING Through HISTORY

People once brewed pee to make an ingredient for gunpowder.

Peeing is a completely normal part of everyone's life. Today we just flush it down the toilet without a second thought. But have people ever thought of using the stinky yellow stuff? Actually, they have.

CHEAP GUNPOWDER

Long ago, gunpowder was difficult to come by. Many people had to make their own. Want to know one of the main ingredients? You guessed it — pee!

After collecting the yucky stuff from outhouses, people brewed it in small containers for several months. Then they mixed it with wood ashes. Next, the mixture was dried out to form crystals called saltpeter. The saltpeter was then used to make gunpowder. It was a gross process, but it was cheap.

PEE IN THE GARDEN

In ancient times, farmers used pee as a plant fertilizer. In fact, some people still use pee for fertilizer today. It makes sense. Nitrogen is one of the main ingredients in pee. Plants use nitrogen to grow big and strong. Unfortunately, the acid and salt in pee can also kill plants. Early farmers fixed this by mixing the pee with water.

Today's gardeners have another use for pee. They use the pee from foxes, bobcats, and wolves to keep rabbits and other critters out of their gardens. The nibblers stay away, the veggies grow nice and big, and everyone is happy.

A PEE BATTERY

In 2005, a group of scientists from Singapore discovered something amazing. They found that pee could be used to make a battery. They first coated a piece of paper with copper chloride. Then they placed it between thin strips of copper and magnesium. Finally, a single drop of pee was added to start a chemical reaction. For 90 minutes, the pee-powered battery produced the same electricity as a double-A battery!

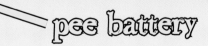

pee battery

TREATING WOUNDS

The ancient Aztecs often used pee to treat wounds. On the battlefield, soldiers would pee on a fellow soldier's wounds to help them heal. It sounds crazy, but fresh urine is sterile. In those days, water was usually very dirty. Pee was actually one of the safest ways to clean a wound. But it's definitely not something you'd want to try today.

GROSS FACT

The ancient Romans used pee to wash their clothes and floors. They even used it to whiten their teeth!

HOORAY FOR PEE!

Running to the toilet several times a day can be annoying. But if our bodies didn't remove waste products, we would die. The next time you have to pee, remember to thank your urinary system for keeping you healthy and strong!

GLOSSARY

antibiotic (an-ti-bye-OT-ik) — a drug that kills bacteria and is used to cure infections and disease

diabetes (dy-uh-BEE-teez) — a disease in which there is too much sugar in the blood

dialysis (dahy-AL-uh-sis) — a process that uses a machine to remove urea and other toxins from a person's blood

homeostasis (hoh-mee-uh-STAY-sis) — the state in which a person's body has the correct balance of fluids and other substances to work properly

organ (OR-guhn) — a part of the body that does a certain job; your heart, lungs, and kidneys are organs.

toxin (TOK-sin) — a poisonous substance produced inside the body as waste

urea (yoo-REE-uh) — the poisonous waste product produced by the body's cells

ureter (YOO-ruh-tuhr) — one of the small tubes that carries urine from the kidneys to the bladder

urethra (yoo-REE-thruh) — the small tube that carries urine away from the bladder; people pee through their urethra.

READ MORE

Goodman, Susan E. *Gee Whiz! It's All About Pee.*
New York: Viking, 2006.

Murray, Julie. *The Body.* That's Gross! A Look at
Science. Edina, Minn.: ABDO, 2009.

Walker, Richard. *Ouch! How Your Body Makes It
Through A Very Bad Day.* New York: DK, 2007.

INTERNET SITES

FactHound offers a safe, fun way to find Internet
sites related to this book. All of the sites on
FactHound have been researched by our staff.

Here's all you do:

Visit *www.facthound.com*

FactHound will fetch the best sites for you!

INDEX